FIVE BAGS
of
GOLD

"the EVOLUTION of CHRISTIANITY"

AC GREGORY

Copyright © 2020
AC Gregory
Kingdom Age Ministries
Five Bags *of* Gold
"the EVOLUTION of CHRISTIANITY"
All rights reserved.

No part of this publication may be reproduced, distributed, or transmitted in any form or by any means, including photocopying, recording, or other electronic or mechanical methods, without the prior written permission of the publisher, except in the case of brief quotations embodied in critical reviews and certain other non-commercial uses permitted by copyright law.

AC Gregory
Kingdom Age Ministries
www.GodsIlluminati.com

Printed in the United States of America
First Printing 2020
First Edition 2020

10 9 8 7 6 5 4 3 2 1

FIVE BAGS
of
GOLD

Table of Contents

Preface 1

Armageddon 5

What Is The Matrix? 9

Leap Of Faith 15

A FALL From GRACE 19

Hidden Figures 23

The Walking Dead 29

The Eyes Have It 39

The Truth Will Set You Free 47

Do You Hear What I Hear? 55

You ARE What You EAT 63

God's Not Dead 77

Preface

"Look at the nations and watch— and be utterly amazed. For I am going to do something in your days that you would not believe, even if you were told."

- Habakkuk 1:5 NIV

On the 18th day of July in the two-thousand sixteenth Year of our Lord, the Word of God came to A.C. Gregory saying, "Go forth and write down the revelations and make known the wisdom that you have been given so that the people of the earth may see what must soon take place." "Sound the trumpet so that all of those who seek the Lord and await His return will hear the call and prepare for what is to come." The Word of the Lord continued saying, "Son of man, you will become a light to those who dwell in darkness and a guide for those who seek the truth. You must speak every Word that you are commanded and you will become a representative to the nations. Pay no attention to those who despise you or those who do not heed your message. The time has come for God's judgment to begin."

First and foremost, this is only the "beginning." The contents of this book are only a brief representation of books and revelations to come. This book is not for the weak. It is not for those who have been deceived by their love for the systems of this today's world. This is definitely not for those who do not love God the Father, nor is it for those who may foolishly believe that Christianity is a pathway to a more "pleasure" fulfilling life. This is a book of insightful, unmitigated truth. I write to those who say "Amen" to the glory of God's impending Judgement while others mourn and lament. I write to those who rejoice in the opportunity to suffer ridicule in this modern world based on their love for our God and Yahshua the Messiah. I write to those who would rather experience death than to be found in disobedience to the Lord Jesus Christ. It is written in the Book of Hebrews that "Jesus Christ is the author and finisher of our faith." It is with this faith and by this faith, and with the grace that has been given to me that I submit to you the revelatory understanding of the present and extremely profound evolution of Christianity.

I pray that in some way, any way, or every way, your knowledge, wisdom and understanding are expanded and that your faith is strengthened and encouraged by the words within these pages. May God's Love and Blessings abound ever increasingly in your life and may God's Grace and Mercy continuously rest upon you as you "harken unto the Word of the Lord" and "discern the presence of the spirit of Christ."

AC GREGORY

Armageddon

"But mark this: There will be terrible times in the last days. People will be lovers of themselves, lovers of money, boastful, proud, abusive, disobedient to their parents, ungrateful, unholy, without love, unforgiving, slanderous, without self-control, brutal, not lovers of the good, treacherous, rash, conceited, lovers of pleasure rather than lovers of God— having a form of godliness but denying its power" - 2 Timothy 3:1-5

My prayer is that you will now open your mind and your heart to the beginning of a journey into revelation, truth, and understanding. Before we dive into the "surpassingly great revelations," (2 Corinthians 12:7) let us first revisit how we have gotten to this point. A brief synopsis of temporal and spiritual history will help to reinforce the revelations of the present and future. With that being said, we begin this journey in the present. This generation has been overcome with "godlessness." This "godlessness" permeates every aspect of the 21st century American society. America in particular has become increasingly more "morally corrupt" since the landmark Supreme Court case of *Engel v. Vitale et al.* in 1962 which removed prayer and the Bible from public schools. This decision of the Supreme Court was the most "spiritually significant" decision in United States history. This decision even represented a stark contrast for a country that was hypocritically founded on many biblical principles, including the plan presented by founding father James Madison of the three branches of government (Isaiah 33:22). Since this landmark court case, American society has become increasingly more desensitized to words and images that are now broadcast and displayed in mainstream media. These same vile and vulgar words and images were at one point considered to be repulsive, intolerable and incomprehensible. In addition, just as prophesied, many people have turned away from the faith and have been swayed by idle notions of "so-called" knowledge-based on futile human intellect (1 Timothy 6:20-21). The "great deceiver" has become the main purveyor of American society as well as the entire world. With the rise of pride, hate, selfishness, violence, vulgarity, lasciviousness, witchcraft, idolatry, and terrorism, it is easy to see that "America the Beautiful," has evolved into "Babylon the Great."

> *"With a mighty voice he shouted: "'Fallen! Fallen is Babylon the Great!' She has become a dwelling for demons and a haunt for every impure spirit, a haunt for every unclean bird, a haunt for every unclean and detestable animal. For all the nations have drunk the maddening wine of her adulteries. The kings of the earth committed adultery with her, and the merchants of the earth grew rich from her excessive luxuries."*
>
> *- Revelations 18:2-3*

AC GREGORY

What is the Matrix?

In the year 1999, with the United States and the rest of the world "on edge" due to the looming fear of a Y2K global shutdown at the beginning of the new year, the Wachowski Brothers (now sisters) dazzled the minds of moviegoers everywhere with their epic title depiction of the answer to a question, "What Is the Matrix?" In the movie simply entitled the "Matrix," lead actor Keanu Reeves (Neo Anderson) finds himself in the position of discovering that everything he had learned, thought, or had been taught about life was merely a computer-generated image of life being maintained in a world that was being controlled and simulated by computers. This world was subsequently and appropriately called, "The Matrix." Keanu, or "Neo" was merely going through life as a relatively unassuming member of society until one day, his life changed completely. In the movie, Neo had been experiencing intuitive feelings that made him begin to search for answers to the question, "What is the Matrix?" There was something in Neo's spirit that was calling him to search for a higher level of truth and understanding. While Neo was searching for the truth and his purpose in life, simultaneously the truth was searching for him. After a string of bizarre circumstances, Neo found himself face to face with the "prophet" Morpheus. Upon meeting Morpheus, Neo was confronted with the greatest crossroads in life. Neo was presented with the momentous choice of whether to take the "blue" pill, which represented returning to his normal life in the Matrix, or to take the "red" pill and learn the truth of the deeply hidden secrets of life on earth and human existence. After careful thought, Neo chose to take the pill of "truth", and the rest, as they say, is history.

"The greatest enemy to knowledge is NOT ignorance, the greatest enemy to knowledge is the ILLUSION of knowledge. It is better to IGNORANT than to be DECEIVED." - Zerubbabel

There is a commonly used adage that chronicles how at times, "art imitates life." Whether it was done unintentionally, or perhaps by divine inspiration, I do not know. However, anyone who has devoted their minds to seeking the spiritual world must concede that at the very least, the Matrix trilogy has spiritual undertones and its plot closely parallels the lives of those who have sought the "truth."

In a way very similar to the Matrix, we unknowingly experience life in two different worlds, on two different realms, within two different dimensions. In the Matrix movies, there is a computer-generated world and then there is the "real" world. In our human existence, there is a "temporal" or "physical" world and then there is the real world, the "spiritual" world that exists simultaneously. In the Matrix movies, people lived life clueless as to the true nature of their existence. This dichotomy also exists in our human life experience.

Just as in the Matrix trilogy, we as humans are born into a world of temporal existence that appears to be real because of the nature of the human "senses" through which we experience it. In particular, the senses of "sight, taste, and touch" are the signature characters by which we are locked into a world that, all while appearing to be "real," is completely temporary and one hundred percent perishable.

Everything in our world that can be seen or touched has "time" stamped on it with an accompanying "expiration" date.

The very nature by which our minds work has caused us to ask questions and seek answers as to the origins of our living existence. Just as in the Matrix, the nature of human existence, coupled with the perfection of harmonious balance within our universe screams from the origins of time, that there is a higher power at work overseeing our existence.

Leap of Faith

"And without faith, it is impossible to please God because anyone who comes to him must believe that he exists and that he rewards those who earnestly seek him." - Hebrews 11:6

Although some men have explored "science" as the means of an explanation of human existence, the overwhelming majority of people submit to the notion that a universe this vast and perfect, could only have been created by a higher power or supreme being. Man's innate, ego-driven thirst for power and knowledge has led us on a quest to resolve the mysteries that have existed since the creation of time… Various answers to these mysteries have been revealed and/or issued throughout the ages. Some have been accepted, and some have been rejected.

As we gaze into the hourglass of time, we can easily understand how one of life's greatest mysteries has always been, "where did mankind come from?"... This question, while extremely "rhetorical" to "some," is a matter of deep thought and exploration for others. This question requires man to confront several perplexing issues within himself and his environment while searching for truth, knowledge, and answers. Man's desire for an answer to this age-old question has always been, and always will be the source of debate until the end of the age. This is because many who ponder this question have a hard time believing in the unseen, even though the unseen is the substance of our very existence. Everything that exists in the natural realm of life, has its origins in what cannot be readily seen with the naked eye. We merely have what we see as the proof of its existence. Therefore, "faith" in what cannot be seen is equally, if not superlatively paramount to faith in what we can see.

Either way, faith can be argued as being the most important substance of human existence. Breadcrumbs of the pertinence of faith in the "unseen" are available to those who will allow their hearts and minds to escape the "self-bubble" created by our egos and to carefully examine life from different perspectives. Air, matter, atoms, electrons, light waves and sound waves, tree roots, and embryos are just a few examples of nature that are invisible to the naked eye. While unseen to the naked eye, these precious examples coalesce into the natural realm to contribute to this perfect sphere of balance that we call life. When applying the same principle to practical existence, our unseen thoughts and ideas manifest into physical inventions. Furthermore, practical application proves that all human life begins with what is not immediately seen during conception and gestation.

The results that are rendered by the manifestation of these "unseen" seeds should create tremendous faith in the principles that apply to these applications.

The exact same principles, with even stronger conviction, can be applied to matters of faith in regards to our Heavenly Father. This is why faith is of the utmost importance. Faith has such high value with God that it has been decreed that the "righteous shall live by faith" (Romans 1:17). This understanding of the "unseen" is the basic foundation of any relationship with our Heavenly Father because God can not be seen. Therefore, any relationship with God must first require the faith that God actually does exist. Consequently, when pondering the relationship between God and Man, it is imperative that our minds are not confined merely to what our eyes can see.

A FALL FROM GRACE

"To Adam he said, "Because you listened to your wife and ate fruit from the tree about which I commanded you, 'You must not eat from it,' "Cursed is the ground because of you; through painful toil you will eat food from it all the days of your life." - Genesis 3:17

It is written in the Book of Genesis that God created mankind in His Image. This gives us the knowledge that we were created to be "spiritual" beings, since God is a "Spirit." At creation, Adam was the essence of God, and perfect like God in all ways. Unfortunately, after an act of disobedience, Adam became separated from God spiritually. In his disobedience to God, the tree from which Adam had eaten made him conscious of himself and subsequently his behavior. The guilt, shame, and condemnation that Adam felt after disobeying God was the result of him falling from "grace." Adam's fallen state was manifested in the fact that his focus had shifted from God to himself. Adam was no longer able to peacefully enjoy the blessings that God had given him because Adam's focus had become self-conscious. His feelings of shame and nakedness that resulted from his act of disobedience were signs of Adam's disconnection from his spiritual nature. Seemingly in the blink of an eye, Adam had changed. Although, according to scripture, God never truly "punished" Adam for his act of disobedience, Adam's fall from grace allowed his mind to be taken captive. This left Adam in a perpetual state of mental bondage that was too strong for him to overcome.

When translated to Hebrew, the name Adam means "man." Man's disobedience to God is the definition of the word "sin." Because of sin, all living things are cursed to suffer death. Thus, the curse of death is traced back to Adam's (man's) disobedience and the fallen mental/spiritual state that followed. Sin and acts of disobedience to God is what allows the earth to be manipulated and controlled by the fallen Angel Lucifer, later to become known as Satan. The fall of Adam (man), whom He had given dominion over the entire earth, is what began God's passionate quest to regain control of the earth. God's desire is to rescue the souls of each member of mankind from the powers of sin and death. This evolution will result in the materialization of God's initial plan, establishing the Kingdom of Heaven on earth and dwelling here with His people.

> *"The mind governed by the flesh is death, but the mind governed by the Spirit is life and peace. The mind governed by the flesh is hostile to God; it does not submit to God's law, and nor can it do so. Those who are in the realm of the flesh cannot please God." - Romans 8:6-8*

Aside from being born disconnected from God, another consequence resulting from the original act of disobedience is that mankind is now born with a sinful nature. This sinful nature is seen through the expressions of our "carnal" minds. Adam's fall from grace resulted in him becoming spiritually blind. His disobedience also begat the awakening of the "carnal" mind. The carnal mind does not readily process that which is unseen and thus life and learning are discerned primarily through our five senses. This subsequently creates a dire conundrum because, as Paul writes in Romans 8:7, "the carnal mind, which is governed by the flesh, is hostile to God and cannot submit to God's Law." The carnal mind, also known as the "soul," is born in slavery to the law of sin and death. In spite of our transgressions, God's unequivocal love for mankind caused Him to set forth an amazing path to repurchase us from mental and spiritual captivity. It is only through the zeal of God and the love of Christ that we are able to reestablish a relationship with our Heavenly Father through the acknowledgment and demonstration of our faith.

Hidden Figures

"So was fulfilled what was spoken through the prophet: "I will open my mouth in parables, I will utter things hidden since the creation of the world."

Matthew 13:35

To even jokingly call God a "Mathematician" is somewhat rhetorical and borderline "disrespectful." The TRUTH is, God is the creator of numbers and therefore His Mastery of numbers far exceeds human logic and understanding. In the same manner in which the Words of the Bible are used to conceal mysteries, there are many hidden biblical secrets that are resolvable through mathematics. Some theologians do not like to apply science to matters of God, however, it can not be understated that God is the Creator of ALL. This includes math and science.

Therefore, why would it not be possible to uncover mathematical and scientific revelations in matters of the spirit? These revelations are designed to unequivocally enhance your faith by formulating bridges over gaps that exist between the mind of carnal knowledge and the spiritual mind of understanding. The truth is, it should not come as a surprise that the creator of numbers would be the master of manipulating them to hide, reveal, and/or fulfill His ultimate purpose.

Just as God has stated that "our thoughts are not His Thoughts, and His Ways are not our ways" (Isaiah 55:8), we must apply the same principle into the way that God views and uses numbers. The most striking anomaly in God's usage of numbers involves "symbolism." Anyone that has a healthy knowledge of scripture should be able to see that God's usage of numbers is much deeper than just what is written. More specifically, God has an affinity for "prime numbers," or numbers that cannot be divided evenly (btw, God loathes "division"). One of God's favorite "prime numbers" is the number "3." The number three in the Bible is one of the numbers that God uses to symbolize "completion" or "wholeness." The number "3" is used 467 times in the Bible. We know that prime numbers cannot be evenly divided, therefore, the number 3 can only be divided by itself. In scripture, we are repeatedly given equations where the number 3 is divided by itself. As it is written in 1 John 5:7-8, "For there are three that testify: the spirit, the water and the blood; and the three are in agreement." Subsequently, we know that the Father, the Son, and the Holy Spirit are all in agreement as one. Here is a trustworthy revelation that deserves full acceptance, this same mathematical principle applies to the Bible itself. The world and the universe were created through God's Spoken Word. This same "Word," after being spoken through prophecy for thousands of years, finally took on bodily form and dwelt among us as a man wearing a coat of human flesh (John 1:15). The man who dwelt among us in a bodily form answering to the name of Yahshua, now translated as Jesus, brought God's Word to life and paid our physical indebtedness so that we can now return to a permanent state of spiritual fellowship with our Father Yahuah. While this understanding has brought us salvation and freedom, it requires a deeper understanding to gain and apply the salvation that has been afforded to us. The first thing we must notice and understand is that everything in creation changes "forms." The Word of God is our primary example. This is an EXTREMELY significant revelation because we MUST understand that the same "Spoken Word" that created the universe, is the exact SAME Word that was born, crucified, and resurrected. Subsequently, this is the same word that we study today and refer to as the Holy Bible.

Transitive Property of Equality: If A = B, and B = C, then A = C

In mathematics, the transitive property states that: If a = b and b = c, then a = c. In other words, if a is related to b by some property, and b is related to c by the same property, then a is related to c by that property.

If "Jesus" is the "Word of God," (John 1:15), and the "Holy Bible" is the "Word of God," then the Holy Bible and Jesus are the exact same things, albeit in different forms. The revelation the Lord has given in this day concerning the mathematical understanding of the gospel is found in the Transitive Property of Equality. This mathematical equation states that: If (A = B), and (B= C), then (A= C). This revelation is extremely important when seeking a higher degree of understanding of the practical application of the gospel. The depth of this revelation requires an open-minded, faithful approach to receive the answer to the solution of this equation.

When we apply this equation to the gospel, here are the practical results: <if> JESUS (A) is the WORD of GOD (B), and <if> the BIBLE (C) is the WORD of GOD (B), <then> JESUS (A) is the BIBLE (C).

> *"It is the glory of God to conceal a matter; to search out a matter is the glory of kings." -*
> *Proverbs 25:2*

This is an extremely vital revelation because it bridges a very important gap in understanding. The understanding of this revelation shifts the psychological perspective more towards the direction of developing a personal relationship with God by the personification of the Bible. This revelation effectively creates a new lens through which Christians can understand and seek a deeper relationship with God. When this equation is properly understood and applied, it sets the course of even the most immature believer directly towards the "Kingdom of Heaven".

The Walking Dead

"On that day a fountain will be opened to the House of David and the inhabitants of Jerusalem, to cleanse them from sin and impurity."

Zechariah 13:1

The thought of death is one of the most frightening thoughts of life for most people. However, one of the most comforting morsels of truth for "believers" is the truth that no one really dies. Our physical bodies wear out or expire and our souls leave their earthly dwelling, but what we refer to as "death" is actually categorized by God as being in a state of "sleep." In some passages of scripture, we see Jesus use these words interchangeably. When we connect the dots of scripture correctly, we find several interesting revelations that give us deeper insight into the death/sleep phenomenon.

In Luke 20:37-39, Jesus responded to being questioned by the Sadducees about "resurrection" by giving us this revelation:

> *37 ...in the account of the burning bush, even Moses showed that the dead rise, for he calls the Lord 'the God of Abraham, and the God of Isaac, and the God of Jacob.'[a] 38 He is not the God of the dead, but of the living, for to him all are alive." - Luke 20: 37-39*

Then again in John 11:11-14, in the Parable of the Lazarus' death, Jesus is talking to His disciples and says:

> *"......Our friend Lazarus has fallen asleep, but I am going there to wake him up." His disciples replied, "Lord, if he sleeps, he will get better." Jesus had been speaking of his death, but his disciples thought he meant natural sleep. So then he told them plainly, "Lazarus is dead," - John 11:11-14*

These scriptures provide us with clear examples of how God uses the words "sleep" and "death" interchangeably. Continuing to comb through the scriptures for other "dots" to connect in reference to these words, we find that Jesus gives us even more pieces to the puzzle in the Gospels. One of the most popular scriptures of the entire Bible is John 3:16. Most Christians can recite this scripture in their sleep.

"For God so loved the world that he gave his one and only Son, that whoever believes in him shall not perish but have eternal life." - John 3:17 NIV

This scripture chronicles the expected outcome for those who believe in Christ Jesus. Jesus offers us further insight into the hope of "eternal life" in John 5:24 where he says:

"Very truly I tell you, whoever hears my word and believes him who sent me has eternal life and will not be judged but has crossed over from death to life."

John 5:24

While these scriptures make a firm distinction between life and death, there are other scriptures that give obscurity to the lines that divide life and death. In the Gospel according to Matthew, a young man informs Jesus of his desire to be a disciple, but he first asks Jesus for permission to go and bury his father. Jesus' response is one that deserves much attention. In Matthew 8:22, Jesus responds to the man by telling him, *"Follow me, and let the dead bury their own dead."*

What makes this scripture so compelling is the fact that we know that "dead" people cannot bury people. Yet, Jesus tells the man to allow "dead people" to bury his deceased father. It would be a natural inclination in today's society to discern the possibility of Jesus being "facetious," however, knowing that "sarcasm" is not readily an attribute of Jesus' character, we must keep searching for a deeper meaning of why these words were spoken. In the sixth chapter of John's Gospel, Jesus gives us a scathing revelation,

> *53 Jesus said to them, "Very truly I tell you, unless you eat the flesh of the Son of Man and drink his blood, you have no life in you. - John 6:53*

Jesus is also called the "Son of Man" and in this passage of scripture, He is referring to His words as His flesh, and His spirit as His blood. Here Jesus tells us that everyone that does not feed on His Words and Spirit is "dead", even though they are still amongst the living and breathing.

The "Christian" faith commands that we must accept Jesus' Words as being "truth" even if we do not understand them.

By connecting the dots and using the framework of Jesus' assertion in John 6:53, we can get a deeper understanding of many Biblical passages that make reference to sleep or death. We now see that in Matthew 8:22, Jesus was not referring to people who were "physically dead" but to people who were not his followers and therefore not "feeding on" or digesting His Words.

This parabolic explanation of sleep and death does not merely apply to the people in the Bible, but also to today's generation of people. We know that sleep and death are both states of darkness and unconsciousness, therefore, we must also process the references of "darkness and light" in conjunction with this spiritual symbolism. As we see in the eighth chapter of John's Gospel, Jesus refers to himself as the "Light of the World."

"When Jesus spoke again to the people, he said, "I am the light of the world. Whoever follows me will never walk in darkness, but will have the light of life." - John 8:12

In the first chapter of John's gospel, it is written about Jesus that:

Through him all things were made; without him nothing was made that has been made. 4 In him was life, and that life was the light of all mankind. 5 The light shines in the darkness, and the darkness has not overcome[a] it."

- John 1:3-5

All of these scriptures provide us with overwhelming evidence in regards to the Biblical "understanding" that anyone who does not possess and feed on the Word of God is walking in spiritual darkness or is spiritually asleep or dead even while they remain in the realm of the "living." We also see this spoken through the Prophet Isaiah through whom God Himself says that,

> "When someone tells you to consult mediums and spiritists, who whisper and mutter, should not a people inquire of their God? Why consult the dead on behalf of the living? 20 Consult God's instruction and the testimony of warning. If anyone does not speak according to this word, they have no light of dawn." - Isaiah 8:19-20

And then again in the New Testament, it is written through the Apostle Paul in his letter to the church at Ephesus that,

> ..... "everything exposed by the light becomes visible—and everything that is illuminated becomes a light. 14 This is why it is said:
>
> "Wake up, sleeper, rise from the dead, and Christ will shine on you."
>
> - Ephesians 5:13-14

As we continue to evolve into deeper levels of true Christianity, there are several elements of truth that must be digested to bring about a paradigm shift in the way that we "think."

We must understand that Jesus' teachings were given to us to be a lamp that guides our minds so that we do not walk in darkness. We must equally accept the reality that there are members of our society that live without knowledge and understanding of His teachings. This understanding allows those of us who are disciples to truly be able to appreciate what Jesus means when He implores us to "cast out demons, heal the sick," and most poignantly, "raise the dead."

AC GREGORY

The Eyes Have It

"For God knows that when you eat from it your eyes will be opened, and you will be like God, knowing good and evil." 6 When the woman saw that the fruit of the tree was good for food and pleasing to the eye, and also desirable for gaining wisdom, she took some and ate it. She also gave some to her husband, who was with her, and he ate it. 7 Then the eyes of both of them were opened, and they realized they were naked; so they sewed fig leaves together and made coverings for themselves. - Genesis 3:5-7

There is nothing more exalted in the entire Holy Bible than the ability to "understand" the lessons of its messages and parables. Even the most intelligent "carnal-minded" individuals stumble when attempting to interpret what the Lord our God has placed before us in His autobiographical instruction manual.

Understanding the Bible requires the ability to see what is not seen. There are very few oxymoronic statements that carry as much applicable relevance as "seeing the unseen." This is a hidden ability that we all begin to practice at an early age, however, our minds rarely cognitively process this ability as a matter of "spiritual skill". Many people will partake in this ability their entire lives and never truly grasp the concept of what they are actually doing. In fact, this ability when misunderstood, undeveloped, and unilluminated by the spiritual mind will often be ridiculed, castrated, or mentally incarcerated in a temporal prison that is unfruitful and negatively labeled as mere "imagination." The positive development of this same basic skill is responsible for practically everything in our daily lives. We owe the building of our houses, the designing of our cars, and the invention of our cell phones and anything else you can name to someone's ability to see the unseen. The "evolution" of this ability in the life of a

Christian is designed to eventually bring us to the realm of "spiritual" illumination. Spiritual Illumination can be defined as seeing the unseen through the light of God's Word. Spiritual Illumination is required to gain access to the depths of the spiritual knowledge and understanding that are found in the Holy Bible.

These teachings are now the evolution of the sacrifice that Christ Jesus our Lord made at the cross on Calvary. As we begin to look at what is written in the Holy Bible through spiritual illumination, we begin to discover some very interesting truths that are worthy of deeper examination. One such truth is found in biblical references regarding the gift of "sight". On several occurrences, we find what are seemingly "paradoxical" scriptures regarding the ability to see. The infallible nature of God's Word insists that we must earnestly seek an increase in our level of spiritual understanding rather than devaluing the Bible's spiritual nature by attempting to reduce the meaning of scriptures to the level of our own limited carnal understanding. When we examine the cliche "seeing the unseen" under this premise, we can easily deduce that although we only have two eyes that are visible, God's Word teaches us that we must have more than just one set of eyes. Meeting at the crossroads of "intellectual reasoning" and "spiritual discernment," it is increasingly obvious that God has blessed us with a pair of eyes that we cannot see. For evidence of this truth, we need to look no further than the first book of the Bible...Genesis. In the third chapter of Genesis, we find the recording of a conversation that would permanently alter human history. What is even more amazing about this conversation is that it takes place between Adam's wife Eve, and a speaking animal referred to as a "serpent." Genesis Chapter 3 verses 1 through 3 records this conversation as follows:

…."Now the serpent was more crafty than any of the wild animals the Lord God had made. He said to the woman, "Did God really say, 'You must not eat from any tree in the garden'? " The woman said to the serpent, "We may eat fruit from the trees in the garden, but God did say, 'You must not eat fruit from the tree that is in the middle of the garden, and you must not touch it, or you will die.'" "You will not certainly die," the serpent said to the woman. "For God knows that when you eat from it your eyes will be opened, and you will be like God, knowing good and evil." - Genesis 3:1-5

This conversation, while remarkable in itself, pales in comparison with what scripture quotes as the direct results of this conversation. We know that the beguiling serpent was being used as a voice by the author of deception himself, Satan. Scripture quotes the results of this beguilement as follows:

..." When the woman saw that the fruit of the tree was good for food and pleasing to the eye, and also desirable for gaining wisdom, she took some and ate it. She also gave some to her husband, who was with her, and he ate it. 7 Then the eyes of both of them were opened, and they realized they were naked; so they sewed fig leaves together and made coverings for themselves"

Genesis 3:6-7

To the unspiritual mind, these verses appear to offer an alarming "contradiction." In verse 6, we find Eve "seeing" that the fruit of the tree was both attractive and desirable. Subsequently, in verse 7, scripture says that after partaking in the fruit of the tree, the eyes of both Adam and Eve were opened. This verse provides a carnal dilemma in the sense that how could Adam and Eve have seen this fruit and other things that are spoken of in the Book of Genesis without having eyes that were "opened" and fully functioning? Through this amazing, parabolic account of the fall of man that God shared with

Moses to be written down for our knowledge and understanding, God is also showing us that mankind is born with 2 sets of eyes. This understanding tells us that we are all born with both "natural" or "carnal" eyes, with which we are able to discern the things of this temporal world in which we live, but we are also born with a set of "spiritual" eyes with which we may discern things that are not seen.

Because of Adam's disobedience, all mankind is born spiritually "blind." What makes this truly amazing is the fact that, without spiritual illumination from the Word of God, we may never consciously understand that we have another set of eyes nor will we realize how blind we are. Without knowledge of the Word of God, we may never access or harness the ability to see "truth" in a world that is based on mere "facts."

The Truth Will Set You Free

"For the law was given through Moses; grace and truth came through Jesus Christ." - John 1:17

A cornerstone to understanding the revelations of God is the knowledge of the difference between "facts" and "truth." Since the fall of Adam, mankind has been relegated to process life through a series of "facts" that are interpreted through our five senses. This is significant because, before the fall, Adam walked and talked with God in the Garden of Eden. Before the fall, Adam's communication with God was not based on optical sensory perception and mental stimulation. This means that before the fall, there was no communication with God by means of the "written" word. Adam's communication with God was solely through the extrasensory perception of God's "spoken" word, also known as "revelation." This revelatory knowledge in itself will prove of great significance as we dive deeper into our understanding of the Holy Scriptures. It was Adam's disobedience to God that allowed him and subsequently all of mankind to be taken hostage by the spiritual forces of evil and also relegated us to the carnal realm of existence. Adam's fall from grace caused him to not only be separated from God, but also removed from the Garden of Eden and forced to learn and discern life completely through his five senses. The enduring result of this fall from grace would cause life and learning for all mankind to come from what has become known as "facts." The word "fact" being a noun, is defined as "a thing that is indisputable." Facts, however, are qualified by our ability to physically see them and to mentally understand and explain them based on our proven knowledge of their occurrence.

Facts are the foundation on which most educational disciplines such as math, science, or history and founded. Facts are qualified by our definitive ability to prove their existence.

Understanding God's Word requires that we allow our minds to not be limited to what our eyes can physically see. Our thinking must also not be confined by that which our hands can physically touch. One of our goals as "Christians" should be to assimilate the Holy scriptures into our everyday lives. In this chapter, we will shed light on several scriptures that will help with the assimilation process by deepening and enhancing your "understanding" of God's Word. Be advised however, that this knowledge and revelation will only benefit you as much as you have already accepted that God's Word is the "truth, the way, and the life."

In the fourth chapter of John's Gospel, we find Jesus having a seemingly "random" conversation with a Samaritan woman at "Jacob's well" in the town of Sychar. It is during this conversation that Jesus introduces us to a prophetic revelation. Jesus speaks to the Samaritan woman saying,

> *"Yet a time is coming and has now come when the true worshipers will worship the Father in the Spirit and in truth, for they are the kind of worshipers the Father seeks. God is spirit, and his worshipers must worship in the Spirit and in truth." - John 4:23-24*

Here in John's Gospel, we see Jesus giving an assertion that draws a distinction between facts that are previously known by the Samaritan woman, and what Jesus refers to as "truth." In these verses, Jesus combines the word "truth" with the word "spirit," therefore we must understand that God's "truth" lies within the "unseen" realm of the "spirit."

We know that God speaks to us in "parables." God's parabolic language requires that the foundation of understanding must begin by processing everything that is written in the Bible with the same question, "what does this mean?" Many people who read the Bible stumble in their "understanding" because of their lack of ability to discern the difference between "facts" and "truth." These are the very same people that Jesus refers to as being "blind." The truth is, we are all born into this world "spiritually" blind and the only cure for "spiritual blindness" is the Word of God. This is clearly illustrated in the 24th chapter of Luke's Gospel where 2 men are walking and talking with Jesus but are unable to recognize Him until He opens their eyes. As it is written:

> *30 When he was at the table with them, he took bread, gave thanks, broke it and began to give it to them. 31 Then their eyes were opened and they recognized him, and he disappeared from their sight. 32 They asked each other, "Were not our hearts burning within us while he talked with us on the road and opened the Scriptures to us?"* -
> *Luke 24:30-32*

God has spoken to us in "parables" as a means of judgment. God did this to separate and ultimately differentiate between those who love Him, (those who truly have faith), from those who are superficial. In the 13th chapter of Matthew's Gospel, Jesus was questioned by his disciples about his usage of parables.

Here we see the question and Jesus' response as it is written:

> *10 The disciples came to him and asked, "Why do you speak to the people in parables?" 11 He replied, "Because the knowledge of the secrets of the kingdom of heaven has been given to you, but not to them. 12 Whoever has will be given more, and they will have an abundance. Whoever does not have, even what they have will be taken from them. 13 This is why I speak to them in parables: "Though seeing, they do not see; though hearing, they do not hear or understand. Matthew 13:10-13*

Understanding the parables of the Bible requires that we first have an understanding of the definitions and differences between the words "facts" and "truth." In Matthew's Gospel, Jesus is quoted as having stated,

"Truly I tell you, unless you change and become like little children, you will never enter the kingdom of heaven" (Matthew 18:3).

The Apostle Paul echoed the Messiah's message in his Epistle to the Corinthians when the Holy

Spirit had him to write, "Do not deceive yourselves. If any of you think you are wise by the standards of this age, you should become "fools" so that you may become wise" (1 Corinthians 3:18). With these scriptures in heart and mind, I beseech you to allow your knowledge and understanding to be strengthened, expanded and ultimately encouraged by these revelations.

Do You Hear What I Hear?

38 As Jesus and his disciples were on their way, he came to a village where a woman named Martha opened her home to him. 39 She had a sister called Mary, who sat at the Lord's feet listening to what he said. 40 But Martha was distracted by all the preparations that had to be made. She came to him and asked, "Lord, don't you care that my sister has left me to do the work by myself? Tell her to help me!"

41 "Martha, Martha," the Lord answered, "you are worried and upset about many things, 42 but few things are needed—or indeed only one. Mary has chosen what is better, and it will not be taken away from her." - Luke 10:38-41

Upon the creation of mankind, God endowed our human bodies with five primary "senses." These five senses serve us in distinctly different ways. Although our five basic senses serve different functions of our physical bodies and although our bodies can survive without either of them individually, each of these five primary senses plays an extremely significant role in our human experience. God makes several references to these senses in the Holy Scriptures. In Genesis 15:5, God references the sense of sight by telling Abraham to "look up at the sky," as it is written:

> *"5 He took him outside and said, "Look up at the sky and count the stars—if indeed you can count them." Then he said to him, "So shall your offspring be." - Genesis 15:5*

Obviously Father Abraham would not have been able to "look up at the sky and count the stars," were it not for the sense of "sight."

In reference to the sense of "smell," it is written in the Book of Exodus that:

> *21 The fish in the Nile died, and the river smelled so bad that the Egyptians could not drink its water. Blood was everywhere in Egypt.*
>
> *- Exodus 7:21*

Here we see the effects that the sense of "smell" can have on the human experience. The Bible is extremely vivid as it illustrates the depths of the deplorable odor of "dead fish" coming from the Nile River. Today we continue to rely on our sense of smell as the often determining factor between that which is appetizing, and that which is repulsive.

While the senses of sight and smell play profound roles in the ways that our souls' process information, the senses of touch and taste are equally as important. The Bible makes reference to these senses in a variety of ways, some good, some not so good.

Parabolically speaking, Prophets such as Jeremiah were "touched" by the Lord and told to speak on His behalf as it is written,

> *"Then the Lord reached out his hand and touched my mouth and said to me, "I have put my words in your mouth. See, today I appoint you over nations and kingdoms to uproot and tear down, to destroy and overthrow, to build and to plant."* - *Jeremiah 1:9-10*

In other places, the sense of touch is written of much more literally as great calamity came on those who improperly touched the "Ark of the Covenant," as it is written:

> *"The Lord's anger burned against Uzziah, and he struck him down because he had put his hand on the ark. So he died there before God."* - *1 Chronicles 13:10*

Subsequently, the sense of "taste" is also discussed both parabolically and literally. In the first Book of Samuel, much is said concerning the eating of honey, as it is written:

> *"The entire army entered the woods, and there was honey on the ground. When they went into the woods, they saw the honey oozing out; yet no one put his hand to his mouth, because they feared the oath. But Jonathan had not heard that his father had bound the people with the oath, so he reached out the end of the staff that was in his hand and dipped it into the honeycomb. He raised his hand to his mouth, and his eyes brightened."* - 1 Samuel 14:25-27

While this appears as a natural or "literal" manifestation of the sense of "taste," there is another popular scripture concerning "taste" that is seemingly parabolic in nature, as it is written in the Book of Psalms:

> *"Taste and see that the Lord is good; blessed is the one who takes refuge in him."* - Psalm 34:8

These are only a few examples within God's Instruction Manual that demonstrate the usage of our primary senses.

With that being said, God has made it very clear that of our five main senses, the sense with the most spiritual significance is the sense of "hearing."

Any true believer that is seeking the Kingdom of Heaven must honor and respect what is written about the ability to hear. While four of our five main senses are "spiritually" limited by external carnal parameters, the sense of hearing is the sense that is most spiritually exalted through it's "internal" independence. Although sound cannot be seen, touched, tasted or smelled, it still affects the mind, body, soul, and most importantly, the spirit.

It is written in the first chapter of Genesis that "God said, let there be light." At that very moment, what we now know as light appeared. It is also written in Hebrews that "all things are sustained by the Word of God" (Hebrews 1:3). Being that God's spoken Word is the sustaining force of the existence of the universe, we all naturally understand that when someone "speaks," we are afforded the opportunity to "listen." The first chapter of the Book of Hebrews reminds us that throughout creation, God has spoken to us on several occasions through His servants and prophets. Hebrews also asserts that in this latter age, God has spoken to us with finality through His Son, Jesus Christ. The entire portion of the Bible that we have come to know as the "New Testament," is based on the Gospel and Teachings of Jesus Christ. Jesus spoke through the Apostle Paul concerning our salvation, as it is written:

> *"For it is by grace you have been saved, through faith —and this is not from yourselves, it is the gift of God—" - Ephesians 2:8*

This scripture is significant because Paul gives us the means by which grace is received...faith. Subsequently, you may ask, "why is this so significant?" The importance of this scripture was actually revealed in 4 epistles earlier in the New

Testament. In his iconic letter to the Romans, the Apostle Paul writing under the anointing of the Holy Spirit gives the primary means by which faith may be built. As it is written:

> *"Consequently, faith comes from hearing the message, and the message is heard through the word about Christ." - Romans 10:17*

This scripture from the Letter to the Romans, along with the scripture from the second chapter of Ephesians, tell us clearly that the sense of "hearing" is imperatively tied and related to the salvation of our souls.

You Are What You Eat

48 I am the bread of life. 49 Your ancestors ate the manna in the wilderness, yet they died. 50 But here is the bread that comes down from heaven, which anyone may eat and not die. 51 I am the living bread that came down from heaven. Whoever eats this bread will live forever. This bread is my flesh, which I will give for the life of the world." Then the Jews began to argue sharply among themselves, "How can this man give us his flesh to eat?" Jesus said to them, "Very truly I tell you, unless you eat the flesh of the Son of Man and drink his blood, you have no life in you. 54 Whoever eats my flesh and drinks my blood has eternal life, and I will raise them up at the last day. 55 For my flesh is real food and my blood is real drink. 56 Whoever eats my flesh and drinks my blood remains in me, and I in them. 57 Just as the living Father sent me and I live because of the

Father, so the one who feeds on me will live because of me. 58 This is the bread that came down from heaven. Your ancestors ate manna and died, but whoever feeds on this bread will live forever." - John 6:48-58

In the above passage taken from John's Gospel, we see Jesus making what appears to be an alarming, abnormal assertion. In this passage, Jesus refers to himself as the "bread of life." What's even more alarming is that Jesus "doubles down" on his atypical discourse by proclaiming that all people that wish to receive eternal life must eat his flesh and drink his blood. One can only imagine the gazes of indignation that Jesus must have received from the cannibalistic interpretations that his words possibly inspired. If a man were to utter those very words today, he would most likely be met instantly with offense, disdain, and consternation.

The words of this parabolic proclamation will only truly resonate with the spiritual mind. The carnal mind can neither see nor understand the depth of the Words of the Messiah. As it is written:

> *"So was fulfilled what was spoken through the prophet: "I will open my mouth in parables, I will utter things hidden since the creation of the world."*
>
> *Matthew 13:35*

It is also written that:

> *"The person without the Spirit does not accept the things that come from the Spirit of God but considers them foolishness, and cannot understand them "because they are discerned only through the Spirit."*
>
> *1 Corinthians 2:14 - NIV*

The God of the Kingdom Age has now provided us with the spiritual understanding to further decode His parabolic autobiographical exposition.

God has now made known to us with definitiveness and finality, the means by which the "bread of life" must be ingested, which subsequently, is also the pathway to the "Most Holy Place."

In this latter generation, the late, great English poet and playwright William Shakespeare is attributed with the popularization of a quote that states, "the eyes are the windows of the soul." While this metaphoric morsel of wisdom is "carnal" in nature, it is a very important "bread crumb" to connecting the dots of the spiritual puzzle. As previously stated, in God's Math, three testify as one. Just as you have the Father, the Son, and the Holy Spirit, you also have the blood, the water, and the spirit. This is extremely important when considering the way that God instructed Moses to set up the "tabernacle." The design of the tabernacle is a reflection of the design of the human body, also known as "God's Temple."

Just as the "tabernacle" consists of three primary parts, the human body consists of three primary parts. The outer realm of the tabernacle is a reflection of our outer bodies. The Holy Place of the tabernacle is a reflection of our mind, also referred to as our "soul," and the Most Holy Place of the tabernacle is a reflection of our hearts, also known as our "spirit." In both the tabernacle and the human body, we can clearly see that God's Math further provides that three "different" parts come together to constitute or make up the "one-whole" part. With that being said, let us understand that eating is one of our most primary instincts. Eating is required for the growth of any living organism, therefore, each individual part of our amazing temples must eat in order to grow. Starting at conception, we indulge in the process of eating in order to sustain our physical existence. Without eating, any organism will cease from growth, become weaker or smaller, and eventually die.

It is with this understanding that we must process the spiritual truth that defines the configuration of the human anatomy and the means by which we feed each individual part. It is no secret that we feed our outer bodies, also known as our "flesh" through our mouths, by the intake of physical food. The human race has become well-trained in the process of producing and preparing food that feeds our outer bodies. Many of us even over-indulge in the act of eating because of the pleasurable experience that it provides. Unfortunately, the same process that gives us growth and life can also cause us harm and death. In the Words of God written by King Solomon in Ecclesiastes, "this too is a grievous evil." The waste of as well as the overconsumption of physical food has become a human tragedy. In regards to matters concerning food and today's western culture, that which gives life also causes death.

Consequently, just as we feed our bodies in order for them to grow, we also feed our minds through what we are able to see and read. As previously quoted, our eyes are the "windows" of our minds. Our eyes are the principal gate through which our minds are fed and "knowledge" is the food of our soul. Having the distinction of being the most highly intelligent animals on planet earth, human beings in general have an insatiable appetite for "knowledge" and learning. From the time we leave our mother's wombs, our minds are constantly gorging on a steady diet of information that enters through our eye gates in order to be processed and stored for usage in our lives. These images are primarily in the form of pictures and/or words. The very nature of this process creates a situation where we most often accept those images and words that are the most pleasurable to our souls and we summarily reject those words and images that we find to be utterly repulsive.

Comparatively speaking, this method of selectivity parallels that by which we feed our bodies. The correlation of these eating processes also provides equal opportunities for pollution. Just as what enters our bodies through our mouths can be subject to toxicity, that which enters into our souls through our eyes can render our minds painstakingly toxic also. Therefore, we must be carefully mindful of the words and images that we feed our minds. A lack of healthy discernment will allow our souls to become corrupted by ungodly words and images that will ultimately have a negative influence on our thoughts, words, and behaviors.

> *"For the word of God is alive and active. Sharper than any double-edged sword, it penetrates even to dividing soul and spirit, joints and marrow; it judges the thoughts and attitudes of the heart." - Hebrews 4:12*

The division between soul and spirit is one that is easily misunderstood. In Hebrews 4:12, God makes this division known as He also gives us the primary dividing factor. It is written that the "Word of God" divides the soul from the spirit. It is extremely important to identify the "spirit" as a living, equal part of our being. This understanding better allows us to process the fact that our "spirits" also have growth cycles that are independent of our bodies and our souls. With that being said, we must now come to the full understanding of the method by which our spirits receive nourishment and subsequently evolve.

Perhaps the most important hidden revelation that God has made known to His Servant in this introduction to the Kingdom Age is the method and process by which the "spirit" of man must be fed in order to grow and thrive. Just as previously stated, our bodies are fed through our mouths and our minds are fed through our eyes.

It has now been revealed that God's grand design for the spiritual evolution of mankind is for us to feed ourselves "spiritually" through our ears. While this may seem relatively simplistic in nature, God has apparently hidden this great revelation in plain sight.

> *"However, the Most High does not live in houses made by human hands. As the prophet says: "'Heaven is my throne, and the earth is my footstool. What kind of house will you build for me? says the Lord. Or where will my resting place be? Has not my hand made all these things?' "You stiff-necked people! Your hearts and ears are still uncircumcised. You are just like your ancestors: You always resist the Holy Spirit! - Acts 7:51*

In the lead up to this excerpt of scripture taken from the Book of Acts, the Apostle Stephen gives a historical discourse to a group of Jewish persecutors moments before being stoned to death. In the scripture above that, unfortunately, sealed his fate of martyrdom, Stephen makes a powerful correlation between the "heart" and the "ears." Based on the

Word of God spoken through Stephen, there is a special relationship between the ears and the heart. This relationship is also well-chronicled throughout the Gospels. Jesus, who also refers to himself as the "bread of life," constantly implores "those who have ears to hear, let them hear." This theme is also consistent with the tenth chapter of the Apostle Paul's letter to the Romans. In verse seventeen of the tenth chapter, Paul gives the primary means by which faith is received. Romans 10:17 states that, "faith comes by hearing, and hearing is by the Word of God." We have already established that Jesus, the Word of God, and the Holy Bible are all one and the same, therefore, I will declare to you again that the faith that God desires from us, only comes by "listening" to the Bible.

In the first Book of Moses, also known as "Genesis," God planted two 'trees' in the middle of the Garden of Eden. Those are the "Tree of Life," and the "Tree of the Knowledge of Good and Evil."

The Lord God then gave Adam the first and only commandment that was accompanied by a negative consequence. Adam was warned that if he chose to eat from the "Tree of the Knowledge of Good and Evil," that he will certainly die. Unfortunately, Adam chose to disobey God and sin was born into all mankind through Adam's disobedience. This greatly illustrates the importance that God has placed not only on the function of "eating," but more importantly, the substance that we choose to eat. This parable is played out daily in every aspect of our lives. God has given us free will to choose what we desire to consume. Just as in the Garden of Eden, choosing to consume the fruit from the tree of the knowledge of good and evil will still bring about the eventuality of death.

> *Jesus answered, "It is written: 'Man shall not live on bread alone, but on every word that comes from the mouth of God.'" - Matthew 4:4*

Fortunately for the Children of God, we can now regain entrance to the proverbial Garden of Eden. By choosing to consume the Word of God, also known as Jesus Christ, we can now take hold of the "flaming sword" that was placed by God to guard the entrance to the Garden of Eden.

Through feeding our spirits by listening to the Word of God, we now have the knowledge, understanding, and ability to grasp this sword and reenter the paradise that was once lost to mankind. By our consumption and obedience to God's Word, also known as Jesus, or the bread of life, we have now been given the opportunity to eat the fruit from the tree of life and thus, live forever.

God's Not Dead

Very truly I tell you, in the year 2020 (on the Gregorian calendar), we are living in the most spiritually significant time since the crucifixion of the Messiah. I wish that I was writing you to tell you to be encouraged and that all will be well with you. Unfortunately, that is not the message that I have been given to share. This is a time where God has been utterly rejected and people have become increasingly un-Godly. This is an age where things that are vile and perverse have become acceptable and things that are evil and wicked in the eyes of God have become normal. We are living in a time where greed and inequality have become the gold standards and the blatant idolaters are worshipped along with their many worldly possessions.

For those who are paying close attention, the winds of change can be heard and felt from every region of the planet. In this culmination of the ages, God has begun to release greater revelations and understanding of the holy scriptures. As we actively witness the transition from the "church age" to the "Kingdom Age," we must understand that this process will not be an easy one. Change is never easy and growth rarely comes without "growing pains." This transition will require us to have a much higher degree of faith. This is especially true for those who consider themselves to be members of "God's Household." As it is written,

> ***For it is time for judgment to begin with God's household; and if it begins with us, what will the outcome be for those who do not obey the gospel of God? And, "If it is hard for the righteous to be saved, what will become of the ungodly and the sinner?"***
>
> ***1 Peter 4:17-18***

This warning alone should be enough to bring Christians to repentance, however, just as children, sometimes more is required to get our attention. Change is never comfortable, yet, it always becomes necessary. The evolution taking place in Christianity is no different. Today's church does not fit the description of Jesus's beautiful bride that is spoken of in the Book of Revelations. Until everything that is written has come to pass, we can continue to expect God's Plan to unfold right before our eyes in stunning fashion. As a servant of the Word, it is a great honor to be given a role to play in this evolution. In the days to ahead, I look forward to serving, sharing, and building with you as the stakes of spiritual warfare will be raised exponentially. According to Hebrews 1:2, God had spoken to us with finality through the Words that have been written in the Bible. God has given us the entire story from beginning to end.

This means that none of us should be surprised by anything that transpires as we move closer to the glorious conclusion.

Therefore brothers and sisters, let us prepare ourselves for the changes that are upon us. Let's prepare ourselves to stand firm on our faith and on the Word of Truth. Now is the time to repent of this world's systems and turn our hearts and minds back to our Heavenly Father. With that being said, I pray through the power of the Holy Spirit with the grace that the Lord has given me, that you will receive the revelations of this book, as well as part two of this book, (the Revelations of Zerubbabel), as what they are...the unabridged, unmitigated, Words of God. Now is the time to be earnest and repent. Now is the time to submit yourself to God's Word and put the love taught by Christ into practice. The Holy Spirit can testify to the undying love that I have for you as these words are being written.

And now to Him who can present you to himself without stain, spot, or blemish, and to make the love of Christ to dwell increasingly, abundantly, deep inside of your heart, to the One True God of all creation be power, glory, majesty, and dominion, on earth and in Heaven, now and forevermore, in the names of Yashua Ha Maschiach and Immanuel,

Amen and Amen.

- Shalom

Zerubbabel

Notes

Notes

Notes

Notes

Notes

Notes

NOTES

Notes

Notes

Notes

Notes

Notes

www.ingramcontent.com/pod-product-compliance
Lightning Source LLC
LaVergne TN
LVHW051508070426
835507LV00022B/2997